This is

WHAT HAPPENED

HILLARY

By: D.K.N. Nielson

2017 First Print Edition
All Rights Reserved
ISBN-13:978-1976529207
ISBN-10:1976529204

This is my story of what happened.
It is not a politician's perspective.
It is certainly not the perspective of a career
politician... like that of the Clintons.
This is one American's perspective.
It isn't that far off the perspective of MOST
Americans. It won't take that long to explain
WHAT HAPPENED most American's know already.
It will be a concise explanation of the events of
the 2016 presidential election, and it will be
more than enough for most American's... this is
because we American's could care less WHT
HAPPENED, we are much more interested in...
WHAT WILL HAPPEN, and WHAT IS HAPPENING.
That being said, I will attempt to clarify this in a
way that an American will appreciate and a
career politician can understand.

YOU LOST THE ELECTION!

Let Me Say That Slower

YOU

LOST

THE

ELECTION!

You' Hillary Clinton

LOST THE ELECTION!

YoU Were not good enough to win.

Your Opponent was better than you.

People Don't Like You!

Bill Clinton...

...your Husband...

...He doesn't
Seem to
like you...

...That much.

You Should be in JAIL!

Benghazi

You Will never Be President.

You will never Live in the White House Again.

YOU
are not
presidential.

You are not very healthy.

YOU have Not helped others.

You
are a
career
politician.

YES...
Career
Politicians
are bad!

This country was not built by career Politicians.

You should
have put in
your political
service...

...Then gone back to work in your field.

BUT WAIT You don't have a field... no regular job.

MONICA LEWINSKY TOOK THAT... NO PUN NEEDED

You are not like other Americans.

You
Are what
is wrong
with
America.

YoU
are actually
quite...

DEPLORABLE

YOU
Blame
Russia.

YOU Don't Accept Responsibility.

It was you

Not Russia.

People Don't Like You.

YOU
are a
joke to
most Americans.

Remember that old bumpersticker?

Back when
Bill and Monica
played hide
the sausage
in the oval office.

"Don't Blame me...

"I didn't vote for Hillary!"

So you
answer
that with
the slogan...

"I'm with Her."

It amazes me
that anyone
was with her.

You pretend
to be so
affected...

but really

Only by

your

bottom line,

THE MONEY

THE FAME

THE PRESTIGE

You remind me of someone.

A character
a cartoon
a movie...

MARGARET WADE

YOU KNOW...

The little girl from Dennis the Menace.

That little
Self-important
know it all.

She Really Likes Dennis.

He doesn't
Care much
for her but
puts up with her.

Sort of like
you and Bill.

She even decided that she would be the first female president.

I guess she was wrong.

Believe it
or not
HILLARY...

AMERICA IS GREAT WITHOUT YOU!

THAT
IS
WHAT
HAPPENED.

www.ingramcontent.com/pod-product-compliance
Lightning Source LLC
Chambersburg PA
CBHW050853260726
48660CB00006B/2607